DEDICATION

This book is dedicated to all parents and caregivers who brave the challenges of raising children with boundless love and unwavering commitment. To those who strive every day to be the understanding, guiding force in their children's lives—your work shapes the future, one child at a time.

And a special dedication to my own mother, whose grace and wisdom in nurturing my childhood journey inspired me to embrace and advocate for compassionate and mindful parenting. Her example taught me that the heart of parenting is built on love, patience, and the courage to guide without holding back the freedom to explore.

May this book offer you support, insight, and encouragement as you continue your invaluable journey in parenting.

ᛩᛩᛩ

Contents

Contents

Prayer

"Om Bhadram Karnebhih Shrinuyama Devah
Bhadram Pashyemakshabhiryajatrah
Sthirairangais Tushtuvamsastanubhih
Vyashema Devahitam Yadayuh
Svasti Na Indro Vriddhashravah
Svasti Nah Pusha Vishwavedah
Svasti Nastarkshyo Arishtanemih
Svasti No Brihaspatir Dadhatu
Om Shantih Shantih Shantih"

This mantra is a prayer for universal well-being, invoking the blessings of various deities for protection, health, and happiness. It emphasizes the importance of experiencing the auspicious through all senses and living a life aligned with divine purpose. The repetition of "Shantih" at the end signifies a deep desire for peace in the individual, the environment, and the universe at large. This mantra is often recited as a prayer for peace, prosperity, and the physical and spiritual well-being of all beings.

ᠱᠱᠱ

About The Author

Dr. Minakshi Bansal, born in the bustling metropolis of Delhi, India, has led a life steeped in artistry, scholarly pursuit, and an unwavering commitment to societal betterment. Following her marriage, she relocated to Ahmedabad, Gujarat, where she has since blossomed into a multifaceted beacon of inspiration for many. Dr. Minakshi is not only recognized as a gifted artist in the realm of Fine Arts but also as an esteemed author, a devoted social worker and a dedicated research scholar in Psychology. Her journey, marked by a profound dedication to elevating those around her, especially the downtrodden and underprivileged children of society, is a testament to her deep-seated belief in the transformative power of engagement and empathy.

From her earliest days, Minakshi was distinguished by an insatiable appetite for reading. Her literary universe was inhabited by characters and narratives that spanned ethical tales, motivational and inspirational stories, and the mythic parables imbued with life lessons. This voracious reading habit was not merely for personal edification but was driven by a desire to distill and disseminate the essence of these narratives to foster the development of students and peers alike. She was particularly captivated by the lives and teachings of historical figures and spiritual leaders such as Adi Shankaracharya, Swami Vivekananda, Dr. APJ Abdul Kalam, Mahamana Pandit Madan Mohan Malviya, Mahatma Gandhi, Sardar Vallabhai Patel, and Vinoba Bhave, among others. Their philosophies and life stories fueled her ambition to embody their ideals of resilience, selflessness, and relentless pursuit of knowledge.

Dr. Minakshi's academic and practical engagement with psychology has been equally noteworthy. As a research scholar, her focus has been on exploring the intricate tapestry of the human psyche, aiming to unlock the potential for psychological well-being and societal harmony. Her scholarly work is complemented by her active involvement in social work, where she employs her academic insights to make tangible differences in the lives of the underprivileged. Her endeavours in social work are characterized by an innovative approach that combines traditional wisdom with contemporary psychological practices to address the multifaceted challenges faced by these communities.

Her artistic talents, another facet of her diverse capabilities, are not merely a personal passion but also serve as a medium through which she communicates and connects with others. Her art, rich in symbolism and emotional depth, reflects her philosophical inquiries and social concerns, offering viewers a glimpse into the breadth of her intellect and the depth of her compassion.

In addition to her contributions to the arts and social sciences, Dr. Minakshi has embraced the healing arts of Pranic Healing, mastering the techniques developed by Master Choa Kok Sui. This practice, which focuses on the manipulation of Prana or life energy to heal the body and aura, has been both a personal journey of discovery and a means through which she extends her healing touch to others. Her proficiency in Pranic Healing is complemented by her advocacy and teaching of various forms of meditation aimed at rejuvenation, personal betterment, and the cultivation of harmony within individuals and communities alike.

Dr. Minakshi's life is a narrative of relentless pursuit, not just of personal achievement but of the upliftment and empowerment of society at large. Her diverse interests and talents—spanning the arts, literature, psychology, and the healing practices—converge on a singular path of service. She embodies the spirit of the luminaries who inspired her, channelling their legacy through her actions and teachings. Through her books, art, and social initiatives, she continues to inspire a new generation to embark on their own journeys of self-discovery, resilience, and altruism.

Her commitment to social betterment, particularly her focus on uplifting underprivileged children, reflects a deep understanding of the transformative potential of education and personal development. By integrating her knowledge of psychology, her artistic sensibilities, and her healing practices, Dr. Bansal has developed a holistic approach to social work that addresses both the immediate needs and the long-term well-being of the communities she serves.

As an author, Dr. Minakshi's writings offer a blend of inspirational insights, practical wisdom, and reflective contemplations drawn from her extensive reading and life experiences. Her books serve as a guide for those seeking to navigate the complexities of life with grace, resilience, and purpose. Through her narratives, she extends an invitation to her readers to explore the depths of their own potential and to contribute meaningfully to the collective well-being of society.

In Dr. Minakshi Bansal, we find a remarkable synthesis of the artist, the scholar, the healer, and the social activist. Her life's work stands as a beacon of hope and a source of inspiration for individuals seeking to make a difference in the world. Her story is a compelling reminder of the power of individual action, rooted in compassion and driven by a profound commitment to the betterment of humanity. Dr. Minakshi's legacy is not just in the tangible outcomes of her efforts but in the enduring spirit of inquiry, empathy, and service that she embodies.

ৡৡৡ

Preface

Parenting, in its essence, is an intricate dance of guidance and growth, a journey embarked upon by many with an amalgamation of excitement, hope, and, understandably, a touch of apprehension. "Guiding with Grace: Mindful Techniques for Compassionate Parenting" is borne of the philosophy that parenting should not only be about guiding a child through the world but also growing alongside them in the process. It is a guide crafted to aid parents—mothers, fathers, single parents, and guardians alike—in nurturing a relationship with their children that is founded on mindfulness and compassion.

My journey into the realm of parenting advice is perhaps unorthodox, as it originates not from raising my own children, but from my extensive career as an educator and counselor, roles that have allowed me the privilege of interacting with hundreds of children and their families. This unique vantage point has afforded me the opportunity to observe a variety of parenting styles and their long-term effects on children's development. It has also enabled me to synthesize a broad spectrum of strategies that are not only theoretical but have been tested in the everyday lives of real families.

Each chapter of this book is an endeavor to distill these observations and experiences into practical advice, aimed at fostering both the child's and the parent's emotional and psychological growth. The core of this book is the belief that mindful parenting is a powerful tool that can transform relationships. It's about more than just managing behavior—mindful parenting involves nurturing a child's mind, understanding their emotions, and supporting their personal growth in a thoughtful and intentional way.

The inspiration for this book came from witnessing the challenges many parents face in our fast-paced, often disconnected world. I saw parents struggling to balance the demands of modern life with the need to provide emotional and psychological support to their children. In my practice, I've watched many grapple with feelings of inadequacy and frustration, which led me to search for a better way to help them reconnect with their parenting instincts and with their children.

Moreover, as a single woman in the field of child development, I have often been met with skepticism—how can someone who isn't a parent possibly understand the complexities of raising a child? This book is also my response to that query. It is a testament to the fact that effective parenting strategies can come from careful study and compassionate observation, and that one does not need to be a parent to understand and convey the principles of raising a happy, healthy child.

In "Guiding with Grace," I share techniques that will help parents:

Set the Foundation: Understand what mindful parenting really means and how it can change your approach to raising children.

The Power of Presence: Learn how being truly present can enhance the relationship between you and your child, fostering better communication and mutual respect.

Listening with Love: Discover the importance of listening not just to the words your child says but to the feelings and thoughts they express.

Compassion in Action: Explore ways to respond to your child that build empathy and understanding, even in challenging situations.

Self-Care for Parents: Highlight the critical role of parental well-being in the family dynamic and how taking care of oneself is integral to effective parenting.

Building Emotional Intelligence: Teach your children how to manage their emotions and respond to the emotions of others in a healthy way.

Creating a Peaceful Home Environment: Offer strategies for crafting a home life that supports all family members emotionally and psychologically.

Each chapter is designed to build upon the last, creating a comprehensive guide to mindful parenting. However, each section also stands alone as a resource on a specific aspect of parenting.

This book is for all parents, whether they are just embarking on the parenting journey or are looking to refine their approach as their children grow. It is my hope that "Guiding with Grace" serves as a gentle companion, a reminder that parenting is not just about steering a child through life but about embarking on a transformative journey that can teach us about ourselves, deepen our capacities for love and patience, and enrich our lives immeasurably.

May this book inspire you to parent with intention, compassion, and, indeed, grace.

ppp

ONE

SETTING THE FOUNDATION: WHAT IS MINDFUL PARENTING?

Mindful parenting is a way of raising children that involves being fully present and attentive to your child's needs, feelings, and experiences. It's about paying close attention to your parenting style and how you connect with your child. This approach helps build strong, healthy relationships between parents and children and supports the emotional and psychological development of the child.

At the heart of mindful parenting is the concept of mindfulness, which is the practice of paying full attention to the present moment with acceptance and without judgment. This means observing your own feelings and thoughts as well as your child's without immediately reacting to them. It's about recognizing what is happening in your mind and body, as well as in your child's world, and choosing your response carefully instead of reacting on impulse.

One of the primary benefits of mindful parenting is that it helps parents become more attuned to their children's needs and emotions. This attunement makes children feel valued and understood, which is crucial for their self-esteem and mental health. When children believe that their feelings and thoughts are important, they are more likely to share them with their parents, leading to better communication.

Furthermore, mindful parenting encourages parents to manage their own stress more effectively. Parenting can be challenging and stressful, and it's easy to become overwhelmed. By practicing mindfulness, parents can learn to calm themselves in stressful situations, which not only helps them but also provides a calm, supportive environment for their children. When parents handle stress better, they are less likely to lash out at their children in frustration, which creates a more peaceful home environment.

In addition, mindful parenting teaches children how to regulate their own emotions. When children watch their parents respond to stress with calmness and compassion, they learn to emulate these behaviors. This emotional regulation is crucial for children's social development, as it helps them handle conflicts and build relationships with others. Children who learn these skills from a young age are better equipped to face the challenges of growing up.

One way to practice mindful parenting is through active listening. This involves giving your full attention to your child when they are speaking without planning your next response or judging what they are saying. Active listening shows your child that you value their words and feelings. This validation is incredibly powerful for children and can lead to stronger bonds and greater mutual respect.

Another aspect of mindful parenting is setting aside time to be fully present with your child. This can be during regular daily routines such as meals, bedtimes, or playtime. During these times, try to focus all your attention on your child, engaging with what they are doing and saying without distractions like phones or television. This quality time is essential for building a strong connection and showing your child that they are a priority in your life.

It's also important to practice empathy and compassion in your parenting approach. Try to see things from your child's perspective and understand their feelings. This can help you respond more effectively to their needs and behaviors. For example, if a child is acting out, instead of reacting with immediate discipline, a mindful parent might first consider what is causing the behavior. Perhaps the child is tired, hungry, or upset about something else. By addressing the root cause, parents can help their children manage their feelings better.

Mindful parenting also involves teaching by example. Children are highly observant and often mimic the behavior of their parents. By practicing mindfulness yourself, you set a positive example for your child. This includes handling your own emotions and stresses in a healthy way, showing kindness and respect to others, and being fully engaged and present in your daily activities.

Of course, no parent is perfect, and it's normal to struggle with staying mindful at times. Mindful parenting is not about perfection but about awareness and effort. When you notice that you have reacted impulsively or without consideration, use this as a learning opportunity. Reflect on the situation and think about how you could handle it differently in the future. This continuous effort to be mindful and improve your parenting will benefit both you and your child in the long run.

Mindful parenting is a powerful approach that benefits both children and parents. It involves being present, listening actively, managing your own stress, and responding to your children with compassion and understanding. By adopting mindful practices, you can create a loving and supportive environment that nurtures your child's development and strengthens your family's bonds. Remember, the goal of mindful parenting is to foster a deep, meaningful connection that guides your children as they grow and learn about the world.

ᗒᗒᗒ

"Mindful parenting is about more than just responding to behaviors; it's about connecting with your child on a deeper emotional level. Through understanding and empathy, we build the foundations for a lifelong relationship built on trust and respect."

❥❥❥

TWO

Being fully present with your child is one of the most powerful gifts you can give them. Presence, in the context of parenting, means giving your undivided attention and focus to your child, putting aside all distractions to engage with them fully. This commitment to being present not only strengthens the bond between parent and child but also supports the child's emotional and social development.

When parents are truly present, children feel seen, heard, and valued. This feeling of being important to someone they love and depend on provides children with a sense of security and self-worth that is essential for healthy development. It reassures them that they are not alone in their experiences and that they have a supportive figure who is consistently there to guide and understand them.

Being present isn't just about being in the same room as your child; it's about mentally and emotionally engaging with them. It means listening to their stories without checking your phone, observing their play without planning your next task, and participating in their activities without being preoccupied with other thoughts. This level of engagement shows your child that what matters to them matters to you.

This practice of being present also allows parents to truly understand their children's personalities, preferences, and behaviors. By observing and interacting with your child without distractions, you can learn a lot about their interests, fears, strengths, and areas where they might need more support. This understanding can help you make better parenting decisions that are more aligned with your child's unique needs and characteristics.

Moreover, being present helps in modeling important social and emotional skills for your child. When children see their parents practicing mindfulness and attentiveness, they learn to emulate these behaviors. They learn the importance of listening to others, understanding different perspectives, and focusing on the task at hand. These skills are crucial for building relationships and succeeding in both personal and professional spheres as they grow older.

Another benefit of being present is that it enhances communication between parent and child. When you are fully engaged, you create a safe space for your child to express their thoughts and feelings. This open line of communication is vital for children as they navigate the complexities of growing up. It allows them to share their worries and achievements, knowing they have a receptive and responsive audience.

Being there for your child also means being there during both the highs and the lows. Celebrating achievements, no matter how small, can boost your child's confidence and motivation. Similarly, offering support and understanding during tough times shows them that it's okay to make mistakes and face challenges. This balance of support fosters resilience, teaching children that they can overcome obstacles and that they have a reliable support system when they need it.

In practical terms, being present can be as simple as setting aside time each day to connect with your child without interruptions. This could be during meals, before bed, or when they come home from school. These consistent moments of connection are something your child will look forward to and cherish, building a routine of meaningful interactions.

Additionally, being present involves being responsive to your child's evolving needs. As children grow, their needs for independence and privacy may increase. Adjusting your level of involvement appropriately, while still remaining emotionally available, shows respect for their growing autonomy and fosters trust.

However, it's important to acknowledge that being fully present all the time is not realistic for most parents. Life's demands often pull attention in many directions. The key is not perfection but the intention and effort to be as present as possible when it counts. When distractions do occur, acknowledging them and refocusing on your child can itself be a valuable lesson in mindfulness and intentionality.

Finally, remember that being present is a practice that benefits both the parent and the child. It not only enhances the child's development and well-being but also enriches the parenting experience. The joy and satisfaction of seeing your child grow and flourish are greatly amplified when you are truly engaged in the process. By committing to being present, you create a nurturing environment where your child can thrive and where your relationship can deepen. This foundation of love and attentiveness is what helps children become secure, capable, and compassionate adults.

ppp

"Every day as a parent is a new page in the unique story of raising your child. Approach each day with patience and love, and watch the narrative of your child's life unfold in beautiful and unexpected ways."

🖤🖤🖤

THREE

Listening with Love: Improving Family Communication

Listening with love is a powerful approach to improving communication within a family. It involves more than just hearing the words that are spoken. It's about understanding the emotions behind the words, the context in which they are said, and the unspoken messages that may be conveyed. This level of listening can transform relationships, building stronger bonds and fostering a supportive family environment.

When family members truly listen to each other with empathy and openness, everyone feels valued and understood. This is essential for healthy family dynamics. Children especially benefit from this approach as it helps them develop confidence and self-esteem. They learn that their feelings and thoughts are important and that they can express themselves without fear of judgment or dismissal.

Listening with love starts with being fully present. This means setting aside distractions like phones or other tasks and focusing entirely on the person speaking. It's important to give your undivided attention to show that you value what they have to say. Eye contact, nodding, and other non-verbal cues also play a significant role in effective listening. They signal to the speaker that you are engaged and interested in their words.

Another aspect of listening with love is patience. Sometimes, especially with children, it can take time for the speaker to find the right words to express themselves. Being patient shows that you are willing to wait, that what they have to say is worth waiting for. This can be particularly important during more difficult conversations or when discussing sensitive topics. Rushing someone or interrupting can lead to feelings of frustration or insignificance.

Empathy is at the heart of listening with love. It involves trying to understand the emotions behind the speaker's words and seeing things from their perspective. This doesn't mean you have to agree with everything they say, but it does mean acknowledging their feelings as valid and trying to understand why they feel that way. When people feel that their emotions are understood, they are more likely to open up and share more deeply, which enhances communication.

Responding appropriately is also crucial in listening with love. This means not just listening to respond but responding in a way that acknowledges what was said. Sometimes, the best response is verbal, such as summarizing what you've heard to show that you understand. Other times, a physical response might be more appropriate, like a hug or a pat on the back, depending on the context and the person's needs at the moment.

Listening with love also means avoiding judgment. When family members feel judged, they are less likely to share their thoughts and feelings openly. Keeping an open mind allows for more honest and transparent communication. It helps family members feel safe to express themselves without fear of criticism or rejection.

Asking questions is another way to enhance listening with love. When you ask questions, especially open-ended ones, you invite the speaker to elaborate and share more about their thoughts and feelings. This shows that you are interested and want to understand more deeply. However, it's important that these questions are asked from a place of genuine curiosity and not interrogation.

Listening with love is a skill that requires practice and mindfulness. It can be challenging, especially in moments of conflict or stress. However, the rewards are significant. Families that practice this kind of listening tend to be more connected and harmonious. They handle conflicts more effectively and support each other through challenges.

It's also essential to recognize when you might need a break from listening. Being emotionally available all the time can be draining, and it's okay to set boundaries and take time for yourself. This not only ensures that you can listen more effectively when you are engaged but also models healthy behavior for other family members.

Incorporating listening with love into daily life doesn't have to be complicated. Simple practices like having regular family dinners without electronic devices can create the perfect environment for meaningful conversations. Encouraging each family member to share about their day and listening attentively to their experiences can make a big difference in how connected and supported everyone feels.

Ultimately, listening with love is about building a foundation of trust, respect, and understanding within the family. It's about ensuring that every family member, regardless of age, feels heard and valued. This creates a supportive environment where each individual can thrive, knowing they have a secure and loving space to come back to, no matter what happens outside the home. This kind of environment is crucial for personal growth and the development of strong, resilient family bonds.

❦❦❦

"Listening to your child with an open heart and mind is one of the greatest gifts you can give. It teaches them that their feelings are important and that their voice is heard, laying the groundwork for strong communication and mutual respect."

▷▷▷

FOUR

COMPASSION IN ACTION: RESPONDING INSTEAD OF REACTING

Compassion in action means choosing to respond thoughtfully and empathetically in various situations, rather than reacting impulsively or emotionally. It's about making a conscious decision to handle interactions with a sense of understanding and kindness. This approach is especially valuable within the context of parenting and family life, where every day presents new challenges and opportunities to foster deeper connections.

When we talk about responding instead of reacting, we're discussing the ability to pause and consider the best way to address a situation. Reactions are often immediate and driven by emotions, which can lead to escalated conflicts or hurt feelings. Responses, however, are thought out; they take into consideration the feelings of others and aim to resolve situations constructively.

Adopting a compassionate response requires a level of self-awareness and self-regulation. It starts with recognizing your own emotions and triggers. When a situation arises that upsets you or makes you feel stressed, noticing how you feel is the first step in choosing not to react on impulse. For example, if a child breaks a rule, it's easy to immediately feel frustrated and respond with stern words. However, taking a moment to breathe and think about why the child might have acted that way allows for a response that addresses both the behavior and the child's needs.

Self-regulation is crucial because it gives you the space to choose a response. This might mean taking a few deep breaths to calm down, counting to ten, or even stepping away from the situation for a moment if possible. These actions help temper immediate emotions, giving you the clarity to think about how best to communicate and solve the issue at hand.

Empathy plays a significant role in compassionate action. It involves putting yourself in someone else's shoes and trying to understand their feelings and perspectives. This is particularly important in family relationships, where understanding each other's viewpoints can sometimes be challenging due to generational or personal differences. By empathizing, you can better appreciate why someone might have acted a certain way, which can inform a more thoughtful and effective response.

Communicating effectively is also a part of responding with compassion. This means not only choosing your words carefully but also paying attention to your tone of voice and body language. Harsh words or a tense posture can escalate tensions, while a calm, open demeanor can encourage a more positive interaction. Effective communication also involves listening actively to others' points of view and expressing your own thoughts and feelings clearly and respectfully.

Consistency is another key element. Being consistently compassionate in your responses teaches children and other family members to expect and trust your reasoned approach. This consistency helps build a safe and secure environment where family members feel understood and supported, even when problems arise.

Practicing compassion in action also includes acknowledging when mistakes are made. Everyone has moments when they react instead of respond. Admitting these mistakes and discussing them openly can be an important part of learning and growing together. It shows that it's okay to be imperfect and that the important thing is to try to handle things better in the future.

Moreover, compassionate action is not limited to addressing negative situations. It is equally important in positive interactions. Celebrating successes, showing appreciation, and expressing love and affection are all ways of responding compassionately to the good things that happen every day. These responses strengthen relationships and create a joyful, loving atmosphere.

Incorporating compassion into daily life can start with small steps. For instance, you might decide to focus on one aspect of compassionate responding, such as listening more attentively or taking a moment to calm down before speaking when you're upset. Over time, these practices can become a natural part of how you interact with your family.

Ultimately, compassion in action is about making the choice to engage with others in a way that promotes understanding, respect, and kindness. It's about responding to both challenges and successes with a heart full of empathy and a mind focused on positive outcomes. This approach can profoundly impact family life, creating a nurturing environment where all members feel valued and connected. Through compassionate action, families can navigate the complexities of life together, supporting each other with patience and love.

PPP

"The essence of compassionate parenting lies in understanding that your child's behaviors are not just actions to be managed but messages to be understood. Behind every behavior is a feeling, and behind every feeling is a need."

🖤🖤🖤

FIVE

SELF-CARE FOR PARENTS: KEEPING YOUR CUP FULL

Taking care of yourself is crucial, not just for your own well-being, but also for your ability to care for others effectively. For parents, self-care can often take a back seat to the demands of family life. However, maintaining your physical, emotional, and mental health is essential to parenting at your best. When you keep your own cup full, you have more energy, patience, and joy to bring to your interactions with your children.

Self-care encompasses a wide range of activities and practices that help you stay healthy and balanced. It's not just about indulgence or taking breaks, but about integrating habits into your daily life that support your overall well-being. This can be challenging in the midst of parenting duties, but it is possible with some planning and commitment.

Physical self-care is one of the foundational aspects of keeping your cup full. This includes getting enough sleep, eating nutritious foods, and engaging in regular physical activity. Sleep is particularly important, as it affects your mood, energy levels, and overall health. While it can be difficult to get enough sleep with young children or during stressful periods, it's crucial to prioritize it as much as possible. Nutrition also plays a critical role. Eating a balanced diet provides the energy needed to handle the physical and emotional demands of parenting. Regular physical activity, whether it's a gym session, a daily walk, or playing in the park with your kids, can boost your mood and energy levels, and it's also a great way to model healthy habits for your children.

Emotional self-care involves managing stress, seeking support, and engaging in activities that bring you joy and relaxation. Parenting can be emotionally draining, so it's important to find ways to decompress and recharge. This might involve practices like meditation, deep breathing exercises, or yoga, which not only reduce stress but also enhance your overall sense of well-being. Equally important is having a support system. Connecting with friends, family, or parenting groups where you can share experiences and challenges can provide emotional relief and valuable insights.

Mental self-care includes giving yourself opportunities to engage in stimulating activities that refresh your mind. This could be reading, learning a new skill, or engaging in a hobby. It's also about allowing yourself time to do nothing at all—simply giving your mind a break. Many parents feel guilty about taking time for such activities, but they are essential for maintaining mental sharpness and emotional resilience.

It's also vital to recognize when you need to step back and take a break. This doesn't necessarily mean taking a vacation, though that can certainly help. It could be as simple as taking a few minutes to sit quietly with a cup of tea, delegating some tasks to other family members, or even just letting the house be a little messier than usual. Learning to let go of the need to control and manage everything perfectly is a critical part of self-care.

Setting boundaries is another key component of self-care. This means learning to say no to demands on your time and energy that are unreasonable or that compromise your well-being. It's important to establish these boundaries not just with your children, but with other adults in your life, including partners, friends, and extended family. Setting and maintaining boundaries can help prevent resentment and burnout.

Moreover, self-care should be tailored to fit your individual needs and lifestyle. What works for one parent may not work for another. The key is to be honest with yourself about what you need to feel your best and to make those things a priority. This might require some experimentation and flexibility, as your needs may change over time.

Incorporating self-care into your life as a parent is not a luxury—it's a necessity. By taking care of yourself, you are not only improving your own health and happiness but also enhancing the quality of care you can provide for your children. Remember, you can't pour from an empty cup. By keeping your own cup full, you ensure that you have the strength, health, and joy to give your children the love and attention they deserve.

ppp

"Self-care is not selfish; it's essential. A well-rested, emotionally healthy parent is the cornerstone of a happy, well-functioning family."

♡♡♡

SIX

BUILDING EMOTIONAL INTELLIGENCE: TEACHING KIDS TO FEEL AND UNDERSTAND"

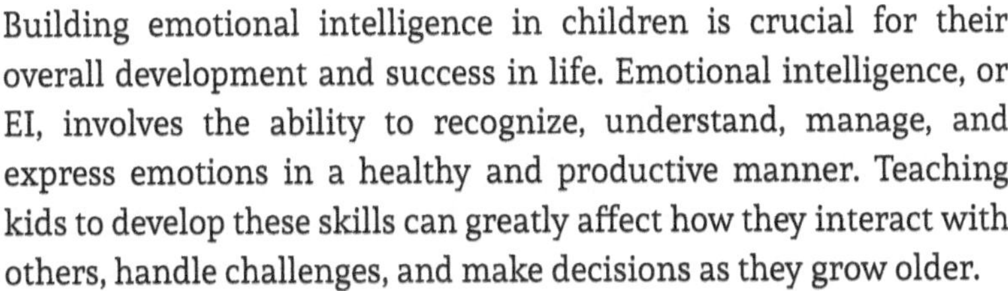

Building emotional intelligence in children is crucial for their overall development and success in life. Emotional intelligence, or EI, involves the ability to recognize, understand, manage, and express emotions in a healthy and productive manner. Teaching kids to develop these skills can greatly affect how they interact with others, handle challenges, and make decisions as they grow older.

One of the first steps in building emotional intelligence is teaching children to recognize and name their own emotions. It starts with the basics like happy, sad, angry, and scared. As children grow, they can be introduced to more complex feelings such as frustration, disappointment, nervousness, and excitement. Parents and caregivers can help by verbally labeling emotions as they occur. For instance, saying, "It seems like you feel upset because your toy broke," helps children connect the word with the emotion they are experiencing.

Understanding emotions goes hand-in-hand with recognizing them. It involves explaining to children why they might feel a certain way and showing them that emotions are a natural response to various situations. For example, a child who is nervous about starting school might be comforted by understanding that it is normal to feel this way when trying something new. Discussions about emotions should be a regular part of family life. Talking about how characters in a book or a movie might be feeling and asking the child how they would feel in a similar situation can deepen their understanding.

Managing emotions is perhaps the most challenging aspect of emotional intelligence. It requires teaching children strategies to cope with their feelings, especially the uncomfortable ones, in a constructive manner. Techniques such as deep breathing, counting to ten, or using words to express feelings are essential tools for children. Role-playing can be an effective way to practice these skills. For example, you could role-play a scenario where a child is angry or disappointed and work through ways to handle the situation together.

Expressing emotions appropriately is a critical skill for emotional intelligence. Children need to learn that while all feelings are valid, there are healthy and unhealthy ways to express them. This includes understanding the right time and place to express certain emotions and learning to communicate feelings in a way that others can understand and respect. Parents can model this behavior by expressing their own emotions openly and appropriately. For instance, a parent might say, "I feel frustrated when I see clothes on the floor after I've just cleaned up. Can we try to keep the room tidy together?"

Listening is another key component of emotional intelligence. Teach children to listen to others and to notice how they might be feeling. This not only improves their ability to connect with others but also enhances their empathy. Activities like asking children to describe how another person might be feeling based on their facial expression or tone of voice can be very beneficial.

Empathy is the ability to understand and share the feelings of another. It is a fundamental part of emotional intelligence that can be nurtured from a young age. Demonstrating empathy yourself as a parent and discussing empathetic responses in daily interactions can cultivate this quality in children. Encouraging them to consider how their actions affect others is also vital. Asking questions like, "How do you think your friend felt when you shared your snack with them?" helps children think about the impact of their actions on others' emotions.

Celebrating emotional successes is important. When a child successfully handles a difficult emotional situation, acknowledge their effort and success. This reinforcement encourages them to continue using their emotional intelligence skills. Positive reinforcement can make a significant difference in how children perceive the importance of managing emotions.

Finally, patience is essential when teaching children about emotions. Developing emotional intelligence is a long process that involves many challenges and setbacks. Children will have moments of great emotional insight and understanding, but they will also have times when they struggle. Being patient and supportive, offering gentle guidance when needed, and being a consistent emotional role model are all critical for helping children develop strong emotional intelligence.

By investing in building emotional intelligence in children, parents and caregivers provide them with tools that will serve them throughout their lives. These tools will help them build stronger relationships, succeed professionally, and navigate the complexities of social interactions and personal feelings. Ultimately, emotional intelligence can lead to a more fulfilling and balanced life.

❧❧❧

"Building emotional intelligence in children is about guiding them to not only understand and manage their own emotions but also empathize with others. This skill is crucial for developing strong relationships and navigating life's challenges."

🐾🐾🐾

SEVEN

CREATING A PEACEFUL HOME ENVIRONMENT

Creating a peaceful home environment is essential for the well-being of all family members. A tranquil atmosphere at home not only fosters relaxation and reduces stress but also promotes positive interactions among family members. In a peaceful home, everyone can feel safe, loved, and supported, which contributes significantly to personal growth and happiness. There are several ways to cultivate such an environment, focusing on both the physical and emotional aspects of your living space.

The first step in creating a peaceful home environment is to maintain a clean and organized space. Clutter and mess can contribute to feelings of chaos and stress, making it difficult for family members to find calm. Simple habits like keeping things tidy, having a place for everything, and doing regular decluttering sessions can help maintain a serene environment. Encouraging all family members to participate in keeping the home tidy not only eases the workload for everyone but also instills a sense of responsibility and teamwork.

The physical design of your home also plays a crucial role in creating a peaceful atmosphere. Soft, soothing colors like blues, greens, and neutrals can have a calming effect on the mind and are excellent choices for walls and furnishings. Natural light should be maximized wherever possible, as it can boost mood and energy levels. In areas where natural light is not abundant, choosing the right artificial lighting can also make a significant difference; warm, gentle lighting is typically more relaxing than harsh, bright lights.

In addition to lighting and color, consider the arrangement of furniture. Spaces that are easy to move around in tend to feel more open and less stressful. Comfortable seating areas that facilitate conversation can encourage family interactions and bonding. Incorporating elements of nature such as plants, water features, or a view of the outdoors can also enhance the peacefulness of your home by bringing in a sense of calm and grounding.

Sound is another element that significantly affects the ambiance of a home. Background noise like traffic or loud appliances can be subtly unsettling, while the sounds of soothing music, nature, or even silence can be profoundly calming. Consider creating a routine that includes quiet time, perhaps in the morning or before bed, to help all family members enjoy moments of peace.

Creating a peaceful home is not just about the physical environment; it's equally about the emotional atmosphere. This starts with fostering open and positive communication. Encouraging family members to share their thoughts and feelings without fear of judgment can create a supportive environment where everyone feels valued and understood. Regular family meetings can be a great way to discuss issues, make plans, and ensure that everyone's voice is heard.

Another important aspect of a peaceful home environment is the establishment of routines. Routines provide a sense of predictability and security, reducing stress for both children and adults. This could include regular meal times, a bedtime routine, or specific times for family activities. Consistency in these routines helps build a reliable structure that can be comforting to family members.

Handling conflicts in a calm and constructive way is also vital. Disagreements are natural, but the way they are managed can either disrupt or contribute to the peace of the home. Techniques like active listening, expressing feelings in a non-confrontational way, and working together to find solutions can help resolve conflicts without escalating them.

Lastly, it's important to nurture relationships within the family. Spending quality time together, whether it's playing games, cooking, or engaging in outdoor activities, strengthens bonds and promotes a sense of unity and peace. Celebrating each other's successes and supporting one another during challenges can reinforce feelings of love and security.

Creating a peaceful home environment is a multifaceted effort that involves both the physical space and the emotional climate of the home. By keeping the home organized and calm, setting up a conducive physical environment, fostering open communication, establishing routines, managing conflicts wisely, and nurturing family relationships, you can build a sanctuary that supports the well-being and happiness of all family members. This foundation of peace at home not only enriches everyday life but also provides everyone with the emotional resilience to handle the challenges of the outside world more effectively.

ၯၯၯ

"Creating a peaceful home environment isn't just
about reducing noise or declutter important aspects.
It's about fostering a space where each family
member feels secure, loved, and free to be
themselves, enabling everyone to thrive both
individually and together."

ᗞᗞᗞ

EIGHT

DISCIPLINE THROUGH CONNECTION: MINDFUL APPROACHES TO GUIDANCE"

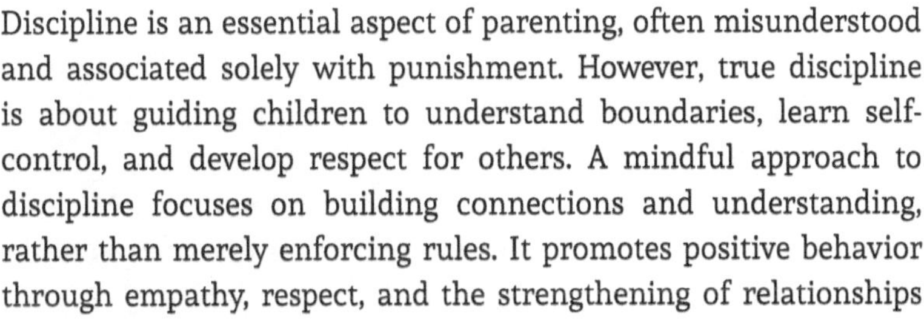

Discipline is an essential aspect of parenting, often misunderstood and associated solely with punishment. However, true discipline is about guiding children to understand boundaries, learn self-control, and develop respect for others. A mindful approach to discipline focuses on building connections and understanding, rather than merely enforcing rules. It promotes positive behavior through empathy, respect, and the strengthening of relationships between parents and children.

Mindful discipline starts with the premise that children behave well when they feel understood and connected to their caregivers. This approach seeks to understand the reasons behind behaviors, rather than just the behaviors themselves. By addressing the root causes, parents can guide their children more effectively and compassionately, fostering a sense of security and trust that encourages cooperation and respect.

One of the key elements of discipline through connection is open communication. This involves talking with your children about their feelings and behaviors in a way that shows respect for their experiences. For instance, when a child throws a tantrum, instead of immediately resorting to punishment, a parent might first try to understand what led to the behavior. By asking questions and listening to the child's responses, parents can often discover underlying issues such as tiredness, hunger, or frustration.

Once the underlying feelings are understood, parents can then explain why the behavior was inappropriate and guide the child toward more acceptable ways of expressing their feelings. This might include teaching them words to describe their emotions, suggesting ways to calm down, or providing alternatives for getting what they want without resorting to negative behaviors. By handling the situation this way, parents not only address the immediate behavior but also equip their child with tools for better emotional regulation in the future.

Another important aspect of discipline through connection is modeling the behavior you wish to see. Children learn a great deal by observing the adults in their lives. When parents handle conflicts calmly and respectfully, children learn to do the same. For example, if a parent consistently uses a calm voice during disagreements, the child is likely to mimic this behavior over time. By demonstrating respectful communication and showing empathy towards others' feelings, parents teach these values directly through their own actions.

Consistency is crucial in mindful discipline. Children thrive on predictability because it creates a sense of safety and security. When rules and the consequences for breaking them are clearly explained and consistently applied, children understand what is expected of them and the structure within which they can operate. Consistency should not be confused with rigidity; it is about being reliable and stable in your responses.

It's also vital to create an environment that naturally encourages good behavior. This means setting up rules and routines that are appropriate for the child's age and developmental stage. For younger children, this might involve removing temptations and distractions that might lead them to misbehave. For older children, it could involve setting clear expectations for behavior that are realistically attainable. By adjusting the environment to suit their needs, children are less likely to act out due to frustration or confusion.

Praising positive behavior is another component of discipline through connection. When children do behave well, acknowledging their effort and success reinforces those behaviors and boosts their self-esteem. Positive reinforcement makes children more likely to repeat the praised behaviors because they enjoy the positive feedback they receive.

Finally, discipline through connection emphasizes the importance of giving children some control over their lives. This doesn't mean letting them do whatever they want, but rather providing choices within certain boundaries. For example, letting a child choose between two outfits, decide what book to read at bedtime, or select a chore they prefer, helps them feel empowered and respected. It teaches decision-making and responsibility.

Discipline through connection is about guiding children through empathy, understanding, and respect. It focuses on building strong, positive relationships where children feel valued and understood. This approach not only makes discipline more effective but also enriches the family dynamic, fostering an environment where children grow into respectful, responsible, and emotionally aware individuals. By disciplining mindfully, parents lay the foundation for their children to develop into well-adjusted adults who are equipped to handle life's challenges with grace and confidence.

ꝏꝏꝏ

"In parenting, discipline should not be about
controlling your child, but about teaching them to
control themselves. It's about guiding them to
understand right from wrong and to appreciate the
consequences of their actions."

ᑭᑭᑭ

NINE

THE ROLE OF PATIENCE IN PARENTING

Patience is an invaluable virtue in parenting, essential for fostering a nurturing environment that allows children to grow and thrive. It is the quiet strength that helps parents guide their children through the ups and downs of growing up. Patience impacts nearly every aspect of parenting—from handling the day-to-day challenges to teaching important life skills.

Being patient means more than merely waiting out a tantrum or enduring a slow morning routine; it's about maintaining a calm and loving demeanor even when things are tough. It involves understanding that children are learning and growing, and that mistakes and slow progress are part of their development. Patience shows children that they are valued and loved unconditionally, not just when they behave perfectly or meet expectations.

One of the key reasons patience is so important in parenting is that children learn how to handle their own frustrations and challenges by watching their parents. When a parent reacts to stress with anger or impatience, a child learns that these responses are normal and acceptable. Conversely, when they see a parent handle a difficult situation calmly and patiently, they learn to emulate that behavior. Children are incredibly perceptive and often mimic the emotional responses of the adults around them.

Moreover, patience contributes to a more effective communication between parents and children. When parents take the time to listen to their children's concerns and questions without rushing or dismissing them, children feel heard and respected. This fosters an open and trusting relationship where children feel secure enough to express themselves and share their thoughts and feelings. A patient parent is often met with a more communicative child.

In the realm of discipline, patience is equally crucial. Effective discipline is not about immediate punishment or quick fixes; it's about teaching appropriate behaviors and understanding the reasons behind actions. This requires time and patience. When parents approach discipline patiently, taking the time to explain and guide rather than simply punish, children are more likely to understand and internalize the lessons being taught. They learn why certain behaviors are expected and how they can meet those expectations.

Patience also enhances the learning process. Whether it's academic subjects, life skills, or social etiquette, learning is a process that takes time. Children have different learning paces, and what works for one child might not work for another. A patient parent can adapt to their child's learning style and pace, providing support and encouragement along the way. This adaptability can make learning a positive experience, rather than a source of frustration and anxiety.

Furthermore, patience helps parents to manage their own stress levels. Parenting can be incredibly rewarding, but it is also demanding and often stressful. Maintaining patience helps to mitigate some of that stress, as it allows parents to take challenges in stride rather than becoming overwhelmed. When parents are less stressed, they can provide better care and a more stable, loving environment for their children.

However, being patient does not mean letting all misbehaviors slide or never feeling frustrated. It means managing those feelings and finding constructive ways to deal with them. This might involve taking a deep breath before responding to a child's misbehavior, or it might mean stepping away for a moment to collect one's thoughts. It's important for parents to find strategies that help them maintain their composure, as this is key to practicing patience.

Patience in parenting also includes recognizing and celebrating the small victories. Every step a child takes towards learning a new skill or improving their behavior is significant. Acknowledging and appreciating these moments can encourage further progress and make the challenges more manageable. It reinforces to the child that their efforts are noticed and valued, which can boost their motivation and self-esteem.

Patience is a cornerstone of effective parenting. It influences how children learn to manage their own emotions and behaviors, enhances communication, makes discipline more constructive, and supports children's learning processes. Patience also helps parents maintain their emotional and mental well-being, allowing them to provide the best possible guidance and care. While it's not always easy to be patient, the benefits for both children and parents are immense. In the journey of parenting, patience is not just a virtue but a necessity.

ᗡᗡᗡ

"Celebrate the small victories just as
enthusiastically as the big ones. Every step your
child takes towards growth is a testament to both
their resilience and your support."

TEN

Nurturing Independence While Staying Connected

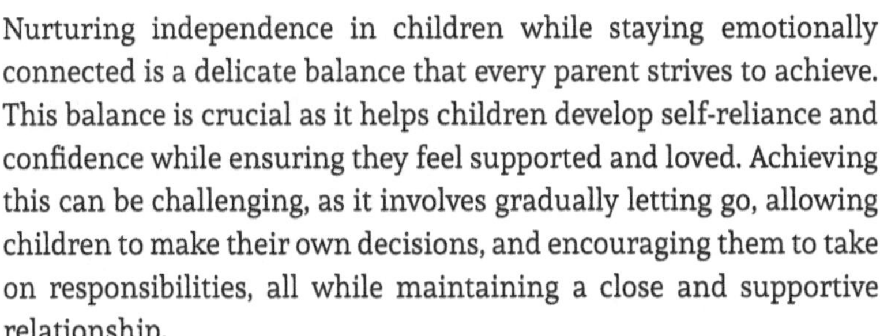

Nurturing independence in children while staying emotionally connected is a delicate balance that every parent strives to achieve. This balance is crucial as it helps children develop self-reliance and confidence while ensuring they feel supported and loved. Achieving this can be challenging, as it involves gradually letting go, allowing children to make their own decisions, and encouraging them to take on responsibilities, all while maintaining a close and supportive relationship.

The journey towards independence starts early in a child's life. From a young age, children can be encouraged to try new things, such as dressing themselves, picking out a snack, or choosing a book to read. These small steps towards autonomy are important because they allow children to experience success and failure in a safe environment. They learn from each experience, which builds their confidence and problem-solving skills.

As children grow, the stakes of their decisions and responsibilities become higher. Parents can support their children's growing independence by providing opportunities that are appropriate for their age. For example, a preschooler might be given the choice between two outfits in the morning, while a teenager might be responsible for managing their weekly homework schedule. The key is to make these opportunities for independence challenging yet achievable, which promotes growth and learning.

At the same time, it is crucial to stay connected with your children. This means being available to provide guidance and support when they need it. It involves listening actively to their concerns and being emotionally present. This connection reassures children that they are not alone, even as they take steps towards independence. It provides a safety net that gives them the confidence to venture further and try new things.

One effective way to maintain this connection while promoting independence is through communication. Regular, open discussions about choices, responsibilities, and life's challenges are essential. These conversations can help parents understand their children's perspectives and provide a platform for guidance and support. Additionally, they offer a chance to discuss the consequences of decisions and actions, which is a critical part of learning about independence.

Respecting children's choices is another important aspect of fostering independence. When children make a decision, whether it's about a school project or a social situation, they take ownership of the consequences of that decision. This teaches them accountability. Parents should resist the urge to step in unless absolutely necessary. Instead, they should discuss the outcomes, whether good or bad, and help their children think through what they might do differently next time.

Setting boundaries and expectations is also vital. These boundaries provide a clear framework within which children can operate independently. For example, they might have the freedom to arrange their study time as they like, provided that their homework is completed and turned in on time. Clear expectations help children understand what is required of them, allowing them to manage their responsibilities independently.

However, as independence grows, so can the emotional distance if not carefully managed. To prevent this, parents can find new ways to connect with their children. Participating in a shared activity, such as a sport, a craft, or cooking project, can be an excellent way for parents and children to spend quality time together, allowing for bonding and the exchange of ideas and values.

Celebrating successes and providing comfort during failures are both essential in maintaining a connection. Celebrations reinforce that parents are paying attention and value their children's efforts and achievements. Comfort, on the other hand, provides reassurance that failure is a natural part of learning and growing, and that the parental support is constant, regardless of setbacks.

Nurturing independence while staying connected involves a blend of encouraging self-reliance and maintaining a supportive relationship. It requires providing opportunities for children to make choices and take responsibility, communicating openly, and actively participating in their lives. This balanced approach helps children develop into confident, capable adults, who know they have a strong, supportive foundation to fall back on. As children grow and navigate the complexities of life, the connection they have with their parents can continue to evolve, becoming a source of strength and guidance long into adulthood.

ϷϷϷ

"As children grow, they seek independence, but they
also crave connection. Balancing these needs
requires an open dialogue, where you listen as
much as you guide, allowing your child to explore
their own path with your support."

ᗡᗡᗡ

ELEVEN

MINDFUL MORNINGS: STARTING THE DAY ON A POSITIVE NOTE

Starting the day on a positive note can have a profound impact on how the rest of the day unfolds, not just for adults but also for children. Implementing a mindful morning routine helps set the tone for a calm, productive, and happy day. This approach to mornings can reduce stress, boost moods, and enhance family relationships by starting each day with intention and positivity.

The concept of a mindful morning revolves around being present and engaged from the moment you wake up. It encourages slowing down and appreciating the start of a new day, rather than rushing through a hectic routine. By incorporating mindfulness into morning activities, families can create a peaceful environment that promotes well-being and prepares everyone to tackle the day's challenges with a clear mind.

One of the key components of a mindful morning is waking up with enough time to avoid rushing. This might mean setting the alarm a bit earlier to allow for a slower pace. Waking up in a calm and relaxed state can significantly affect one's mood and outlook for the day. It's beneficial to wake children up gently, perhaps with a soft touch or a warm greeting, rather than abruptly. This gentle start helps ease them into the day and can make them more cooperative and cheerful.

Once everyone is awake, engaging in a family activity that promotes mindfulness is a great way to connect and set a positive tone. This could be as simple as sharing breakfast without the distraction of phones or television. Breakfast provides an excellent opportunity for family members to discuss their plans for the day, share any concerns or hopes, and offer support and encouragement to each other. This meal becomes not just about nourishing the body, but also about strengthening family bonds.

Physical activity is another important element of a mindful morning. Even a short walk, stretching session, or yoga routine can invigorate the body and clear the mind. Exercise releases endorphins, which have mood-lifting properties. When done as a family, morning physical activity can be fun and energizing, setting a lively and positive mood for the day.

Mindfulness exercises such as meditation or deep-breathing exercises can also be very effective in starting the day right. Even just a few minutes of meditation can reduce stress and increase concentration and peace of mind. Teaching children simple meditation techniques or encouraging them to take a few deep breaths before they start their day can help them develop habits that promote mental health and emotional resilience.

Visualization is another powerful tool for starting the day positively. Encourage family members to spend a few moments visualizing what they want the day to look like. This can help set intentions and align actions with goals. Children can be encouraged to think about what they are looking forward to or what they hope to achieve during the day. This positive thinking can boost their confidence and motivation.

It's also beneficial to incorporate some form of creative expression into the morning routine. Whether it's writing in a journal, drawing, or playing music, creative activities can help express emotions and clear the mind. For children, this can be a playful and joyful way to start the day, and for adults, it can be a therapeutic exercise that helps prepare mentally and emotionally for the day.

Lastly, practicing gratitude in the morning can significantly impact the day's outlook. Taking a moment to reflect on what you're grateful for can shift focus from what is lacking to what is abundant. Encouraging children to think about what they are thankful for each morning can cultivate a habit of appreciation and positivity.

Starting the day on a positive note with a mindful morning routine offers numerous benefits. It sets a calm, positive tone for the day, reduces morning stress, and helps align the day's actions with intentional goals. For families, mindful mornings can enhance connections, improve communication, and foster a supportive and loving environment. Over time, these mornings build a foundation of positivity and mindfulness that can extend into all areas of life, promoting overall well-being and happiness.

ppp

"True patience in parenting comes from understanding that each child develops on their own timeline. Celebrate where they are, not where you think they should be, and trust that they will reach their milestones in their own time."

❧❧❧

TWELVE

BEDTIME ROUTINES: ENDING THE DAY WITH SERENITY

Ending the day with serenity through a structured bedtime routine is essential for both children and adults. A calming end to the day not only helps in winding down but also sets the stage for a good night's sleep, which is crucial for overall health and well-being. An effective bedtime routine can ease the transition from the day's activities to restful sleep, helping family members relax and recharge.

A bedtime routine starts with establishing a consistent schedule. Going to bed at the same time every night helps regulate the body's internal clock, making it easier to fall asleep and wake up naturally. For children especially, a regular bedtime eliminates the guesswork about when they will be expected to go to sleep, which can reduce bedtime resistance and anxiety.

The activities that make up a bedtime routine are just as important as the timing. These activities should promote relaxation and signal to the body that it's time to slow down. A good routine might include several steps, each contributing to a calm and restful end to the day.

One of the first steps in a nighttime routine could be tidying up. Encouraging children to help put away toys and books not only teaches responsibility but also helps clear the physical and mental clutter. A tidy space can enhance feelings of calmness and control, which are conducive to relaxation.

After tidying, a warm bath or shower can be a great next step. The warmth helps relax muscles and lower body temperature, which naturally signals to the body that it's time to wind down. For children, the bath can also be a time for some playful but calming interactions with parents, which can strengthen bonds and provide a sense of security before bed.

Following the bath, changing into pajamas and engaging in some form of quiet activity can further enhance relaxation. Reading a book is a popular choice for a bedtime activity because it allows for quiet, focused time away from the stimulating screens of televisions, computers, and smartphones. For children, bedtime stories are not only soothing but also promote literacy and foster imagination.

In addition to reading, incorporating mindfulness or relaxation exercises can be beneficial. Techniques such as deep breathing, gentle stretching, or guided imagery can help clear the mind and relax the body. These practices are particularly useful for those who may have trouble falling asleep due to anxiety or busy minds.

Another key component of a bedtime routine is a discussion of the day's events or a plan for the next day. This can be a quiet time for children to talk about what they did, what they learned, or what may be worrying them. For adults, it might involve a brief period of journaling or meditation. Addressing these thoughts before bed can help prevent them from disrupting sleep.

Creating an environment conducive to sleep is also critical. This involves more than just a comfortable bed. The sleeping environment should be cool, dark, and quiet. Using blackout curtains, eye masks, or white noise machines can help create an ideal sleeping atmosphere. Additionally, making sure the mattress and pillows are comfortable and supportive can make a significant difference in sleep quality.

Finally, expressing gratitude or prayers can be a soothing way to end the day. Taking a moment to reflect on what one is thankful for can shift the focus from the day's stresses to its positives. For many, this can be a deeply relaxing way to end the day, instilling a sense of peace and contentment.

A bedtime routine that promotes relaxation and readiness for sleep can profoundly impact one's quality of life. By ending the day with serenity, individuals are more likely to have restorative sleep, which is crucial for physical and mental health. For children, a consistent and calming routine not only helps in developing good sleep habits but also provides a sense of security and stability. Over time, these routines can help alleviate stress, improve relationships, and foster a general sense of well-being, making them a valuable practice for anyone looking to enhance their nightly rest.

ᑭᑭᑭ

"Reflecting on your parenting journey is like looking through a detailed map of where you've been and where you're heading. It helps you navigate better, making informed decisions based on past experiences and future aspirations."

❥❥❥

THIRTEEN

DEALING WITH TANTRUMS AND TEARS MINDFULLY

Dealing with tantrums and tears is a challenge that every parent faces. These emotional outbursts can test the patience of even the most understanding adults. However, approaching such moments mindfully can transform them from episodes of stress into opportunities for teaching important emotional regulation skills and deepening the parent-child relationship.

When a child throws a tantrum or bursts into tears, it's often because they are overwhelmed by their emotions and don't yet have the skills to manage them effectively. Young children, in particular, are still learning how to interpret and respond to the complex world around them. They may experience frustrations that they can't easily express with words, leading to outbursts as their way of communicating distress.

The first step in dealing with these situations mindfully is to stay calm yourself. When a parent reacts to a tantrum with anger or frustration, it can escalate the child's distress. Instead, taking a deep breath and maintaining your composure can help create an environment of calm that signals to your child that their feelings can be managed. By modeling calmness, you teach your child that while their feelings are valid, there are peaceful ways to cope with them.

Once you are calm, acknowledge your child's feelings. This doesn't mean you have to agree with their reasons for being upset, but simply recognizing their emotions can be incredibly validating for a child. For instance, saying something like, "I see that you are very upset because you can't have the toy you want right now," lets them know that you understand their feelings. This recognition can help deescalate the situation, as feeling understood can reduce the intensity of their emotions.

After acknowledging their feelings, help guide your child through the experience. This involves encouraging them to express what they're feeling and why, if they're old enough to articulate it. Ask gentle questions that lead them to reflect on their feelings and encourage them to use words to describe their emotions. This practice helps build their emotional vocabulary, which is crucial for emotional development.

It's also beneficial to teach children calming techniques they can use when they feel overwhelmed. Techniques like deep breathing, counting to ten, or retreating to a quiet space can be effective. You can practice these techniques together during calm moments so that they become familiar tools your child can draw on when needed. Over time, these strategies can empower your child to manage their reactions on their own, fostering a sense of competence and self-control.

Providing comfort and reassurance is another essential aspect of dealing with tantrums and tears mindfully. Sometimes, a hug or a few comforting words are all a child needs to feel better. Physical comfort can be very effective in providing a safe space for children to express their emotions and recover from them.

Setting boundaries is also important. While it's crucial to validate and comfort your child, it's equally important to maintain clear and consistent rules. After the emotional storm has passed, gently remind your child of the behavior that is expected and the consequences of their actions. This can help them understand the impact of their behavior and learn to express their emotions in more appropriate ways.

Lastly, reflect on these incidents with your child when they are calm. Discuss what happened and explore better ways to handle similar situations in the future. This reflection can enhance their understanding and give them practical ideas on how they can react differently next time.

Dealing with tantrums and tears mindfully is about more than just managing these challenging moments. It's about using them as opportunities to teach children how to handle their emotions effectively. By remaining calm, acknowledging their feelings, guiding them through their emotional experiences, teaching them calming techniques, and reflecting on the incidents, parents can help their children develop emotional intelligence and resilience. This approach not only makes handling future tantrums easier but also strengthens the emotional bond between parent and child, building a foundation of trust and mutual respect.

ফফফ

"Handling stress as a family unit does not mean shielding your children from every problem, but rather showing them healthy ways to cope with life's challenges. This shared resilience strengthens your family's bond."

♥♥♥

FOURTEEN

THE IMPORTANCE OF PLAY: MINDFUL ENGAGEMENT

Play is a fundamental aspect of childhood, serving as a critical tool for development in multiple domains, including physical, social, emotional, and cognitive growth. Engaging mindfully in play means not just allowing children time to play, but also understanding and actively participating in this play when appropriate. This mindful engagement can significantly enhance the benefits of play, providing children with richer experiences and deeper learning opportunities.

From the moment babies start to reach out and explore their surroundings, play begins to serve as a pathway to learning. It's through play that children learn to interact with their world. They test theories, solve problems, develop fine motor skills, and learn how to communicate with others. For instance, when toddlers stack blocks, they are not just playing; they are understanding shapes, experimenting with balance, and learning about gravity and spatial relationships.

Mindful engagement in play involves more than supervising children; it requires parents and caregivers to be present and involved, observing and responding to the cues children give during play. This could mean participating in a game, helping to construct a puzzle, or simply talking about what the child is doing as they play alone. By engaging in this way, adults help deepen the child's understanding and enjoyment of the activity.

When parents join in with children's play, it offers valuable teaching moments. For example, during a game of make-believe, a parent can introduce concepts such as turn-taking, fair play, and empathy by modeling these behaviors. This also provides an opportunity to see the world from the child's perspective, which can be enlightening for understanding their thoughts and feelings. Engaging with children in play allows adults to teach them how to handle emotions and interact with others in a safe and controlled environment.

Play also offers a unique opportunity to strengthen the bond between child and parent. Shared laughter and joy during play contribute to a deeper connection and mutual trust. This emotional bond is crucial for a child's secure attachment, which is linked to healthier social relationships and better emotional regulation as they grow.

Mindful engagement in play also means creating environments that encourage diverse types of play. This includes providing a variety of toys and materials that stimulate different aspects of development. For example, puzzles and building blocks enhance problem-solving and motor skills, while dress-up clothes and dolls can be tools for imaginative play that develops social skills and empathy. Moreover, it's important to create spaces where children feel safe to explore and express themselves through play without undue restrictions or excessive interference.

The outdoors is another critical environment for play. Outdoor play not only stimulates physical activity but also connects children with nature. Activities like running, climbing, and playing sports are vital for physical health, promoting cardiovascular fitness, strength, and coordination. Additionally, interacting with natural environments can stimulate all the senses and promote curiosity and scientific thinking.

Mindful engagement also means recognizing when to step back and let children lead their play. This autonomy is crucial for fostering creativity and confidence. Children who are given the freedom to direct their own play experiences learn decision-making skills and develop a sense of independence. Watching attentively from the sidelines and being available if needed provides a safety net that lets children explore and experiment with confidence.

Furthermore, play is not just for children. Adults, too, benefit from play. It can be a stress reliever and a source of joy, as well as a way to reconnect with the simplicity and creativity of childhood. Parents who play with their children often find that it rekindles their own creativity and helps them see the world in new ways.

The importance of play in childhood development cannot be overstated. Play is not merely a way to pass the time; it is a critical component of learning and growth. Mindful engagement in play by parents enhances these benefits, deepening the developmental impacts and strengthening the emotional bonds between parents and children. By being actively involved in children's play, parents not only contribute to their children's growth but also enrich their own lives, making play a valuable activity for the entire family.

ϷϷϷ

"Teaching gratitude and generosity is about more
than fostering social etiquette; it's about cultivating
a heart that sees and responds to the needs of
others, enriching both your child's life and the lives
of those around them."

♡♡♡

FIFTEEN

MINDFUL EATING: PROMOTING HEALTHY RELATIONSHIPS WITH FOOD

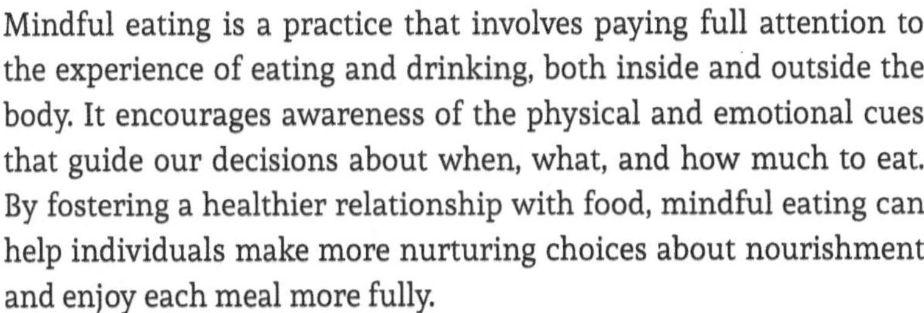

Mindful eating is a practice that involves paying full attention to the experience of eating and drinking, both inside and outside the body. It encourages awareness of the physical and emotional cues that guide our decisions about when, what, and how much to eat. By fostering a healthier relationship with food, mindful eating can help individuals make more nurturing choices about nourishment and enjoy each meal more fully.

The practice of mindful eating starts with understanding the motivations behind our food choices. Often, people eat out of boredom, stress, or habit rather than hunger. Mindful eating teaches us to pause before eating and ask ourselves why we are reaching for food. Is it true physical hunger, or is it emotional hunger? This pause can help break the cycle of mindless eating that leads to overeating and poor food choices.

Once the motivation is clear, the next step in mindful eating is to savor the food. This means taking the time to really taste each bite, noticing the texture, flavor, and aroma of the food. Eating slowly allows the body time to recognize when it is full, reducing the likelihood of overeating. It also increases the enjoyment of the meal, as the full range of sensory experiences is acknowledged and appreciated.

Mindful eating also involves making conscious choices about what to eat. This can mean choosing foods that are both pleasing to the taste and nourishing to the body. A mindful eater thinks about where the food comes from, how it is prepared, and what health benefits it offers. This awareness can lead to healthier choices, such as opting for whole, unprocessed foods over pre-packaged or fast food options.

Creating a conducive eating environment is another aspect of mindful eating. This means removing distractions such as TV, phones, or overly stimulating conversations during meals. By focusing solely on the meal, individuals can better listen to their bodies and enjoy the company of those around them if they are sharing the meal. Eating in a calm, peaceful environment can enhance the mindfulness of the meal, making it easier to be fully present.

Incorporating gratitude into mealtime is another facet of mindful eating. Taking a moment to think about the labor that went into producing the meal—from the farmers who grew the food, to the cooks who prepared it—can foster a deeper appreciation for the food. This gratitude can transform eating from a mundane task to a reflective, enjoyable experience that nourishes both the body and the soul.

For families, teaching children mindful eating practices can be particularly beneficial. Children are naturally more attuned to their hunger cues and can benefit from continuing this intuitive eating as they grow. Parents can teach mindful eating by involving children in food preparation, encouraging them to consider the colors, smells, and textures of food, and by setting an example through their own eating habits. Discussions about how different foods affect the body and mood can also help children make healthier choices.

However, like any practice, mindful eating takes time to develop. It's not about perfection but about making more conscious choices more often. Starting small, such as one mindful meal a week, can gradually lead to more significant changes in eating habits. Over time, mindful eating can become a natural part of daily life.

Mindful eating is a transformative practice that can dramatically improve our relationship with food. It encourages a deeper connection to our meals and our bodies, leading to better health choices and greater satisfaction with our food. By eating mindfully, we nourish our bodies more effectively and enjoy the pleasures of eating fully, which can contribute to a more balanced and joyful life.

"Mindful mornings set the tone for the day. Taking a few moments to breathe, plan, and connect before the day begins can make all the difference in the world, both for you and for your child."

ᐅᐅᐅ

SIXTEEN

HANDLING STRESS TOGETHER: TECHNIQUES FOR THE WHOLE FAMILY

Handling stress is a crucial skill for families, as it directly impacts the overall happiness and health of the household. Stress can arise from many sources, including work, school, relationships, and daily responsibilities. However, when families learn to manage stress together, they can not only mitigate its effects but also strengthen their bonds. Here are several effective techniques that families can use to manage stress collectively.

The first step in managing stress together is open communication. Stress often builds up when feelings are not expressed and conflicts are left unresolved. By encouraging open dialogue about stressors, families can address issues before they escalate. This can involve regular family meetings where each member is encouraged to share their feelings and concerns without fear of judgment. During these discussions, it's crucial for everyone to practice active listening, which means focusing fully on the speaker, acknowledging their feelings, and responding thoughtfully.

Another effective technique is to establish routines that include stress-reducing activities. Routines provide a sense of predictability and control, which can be comforting during times of stress. These activities might include physical exercise, which is known for reducing stress and improving mood. Families can schedule regular walks, bike rides, or visits to the park. Not only do these activities encourage healthy living, but they also provide opportunities for casual conversations and enjoyable family time that can alleviate stress.

Mindfulness and relaxation techniques are also valuable tools for managing stress. These can include practices such as meditation, deep breathing exercises, or yoga. Even young children can learn simple mindfulness exercises, like focusing on their breathing or engaging in guided imagery. Setting aside a few minutes each day for these activities can significantly reduce stress levels in the home. Families can practice these techniques together, perhaps in the morning or before bedtime, to reinforce a calm and peaceful environment.

Shared hobbies and interests provide another avenue for relieving stress. Whether it's cooking, gardening, crafting, or playing music, engaging in a hobby together can be a great way to relax and bond. These activities offer a distraction from daily stressors and allow family members to connect in a positive, non-stressful context. It's also a chance for each family member to express themselves creatively, which is often therapeutic.

In addition to proactive stress management techniques, it's essential to create a supportive environment where family members feel they can rely on each other. This means being empathetic to each other's struggles and offering help when needed. Sometimes, simply knowing that support is available can significantly reduce an individual's stress levels.

Moreover, laughter and play are natural stress relievers. Families should not overlook the importance of fun and humor in their daily lives. Watching a funny movie, telling jokes, or playing games can lighten the atmosphere and improve everyone's mood.

It's also important for families to learn how to manage their time effectively. Poor time management can lead to a lot of stress, especially in busy households. Together, families can set priorities, delegate tasks, and establish schedules that allow sufficient time for both responsibilities and relaxation. This planning can help reduce the chaos and rush that often contribute to stress.

Lastly, every family member must have some personal time. While it's beneficial to handle stress together, individual time for relaxation and introspection is also crucial. Each family member should have the opportunity to pursue activities they enjoy independently, which helps them recharge and maintain their mental health.

Handling stress as a family involves a combination of open communication, shared activities, supportive interactions, and personal time. By adopting these techniques, families can not only manage stress more effectively but also enhance their relationships with one another. These practices can help ensure that the home is a sanctuary where all members feel valued, supported, and, most importantly, calm.

᠉᠉᠉

"When you teach a child to eat mindfully, you're not just teaching them healthy eating habits. You're showing them how to be present and fully enjoy every aspect of life, one moment at a time."

ᗗᗗᗗ

SEVENTEEN

Teaching Gratitude and Generosity

Teaching gratitude and generosity is a vital aspect of parenting that helps children develop into caring, empathetic, and socially responsible adults. These values not only contribute to the happiness and well-being of others but also enhance the personal satisfaction and fulfillment of those who practice them. Cultivating an attitude of gratitude and a spirit of generosity can start early in childhood and continue throughout life, providing significant benefits along the way.

Gratitude involves recognizing and appreciating what one has, rather than focusing solely on what one desires. It extends to acknowledging the efforts of others that benefit one's life. Teaching children to be grateful helps them develop a positive perspective, fostering happiness and resilience against life's challenges. Generosity, the act of giving freely without expecting anything in return, reinforces social bonds and promotes a sense of community and connection.

One effective way to teach these values is through modeling. Children learn a great deal from observing the actions of adults, particularly their parents. When children see their parents expressing thanks regularly or sharing resources and time with others, they are more likely to adopt these behaviors themselves. Parents can demonstrate gratitude by verbally expressing thanks for everyday comforts and kindnesses, discussing the good things that happen each day, and writing thank-you notes for gifts and gestures. Similarly, they can show generosity by donating to the less fortunate, volunteering their time, and sharing resources with friends and neighbors.

Another powerful method is through direct teaching. Parents can encourage children to express gratitude by asking them to think of things they are thankful for each day. This can be part of a daily routine, such as during meal times or before bed. Discussing why they are thankful for these things can deepen their understanding and appreciation. For teaching generosity, parents can involve children in selecting toys or clothes to donate or encourage them to share with siblings and friends. These actions help children experience the joy of giving and understand the positive impact of generosity on others.

Reading stories and books that illustrate gratitude and generosity is also an educational tool. Many children's books feature themes of thankfulness and acts of kindness that can inspire children and provide concrete examples of how these virtues can be practiced. Discussing these stories and relating them to real-life situations can help solidify these lessons.

Encouraging reflection on the feelings associated with gratitude and generosity can also enhance understanding. After a child expresses thanks or gives something to someone, parents can discuss how it made the child feel. Likely, the feelings will be positive, reinforcing the behavior. It's also helpful to talk about how the recipient might feel, which can develop empathy and further motivate generous and grateful actions.

Recognizing and praising genuine displays of gratitude and generosity can reinforce these behaviors. Positive reinforcement makes children feel good about their actions and more likely to repeat them. However, it's important that the praise is specific and sincere, focusing on the effort and thought behind the action rather than the action alone.

Creating traditions around gratitude and generosity can also solidify these values within the family. This might include volunteer days with the whole family, making and delivering gifts during holidays, or maintaining a gratitude journal where family members can write down things they are thankful for. These traditions not only make the practices regular but also fun and memorable.

Finally, discussing the broader impacts of gratitude and generosity can help children understand why these values are important. Explaining how gratitude can make life more enjoyable or how generosity can improve someone else's circumstances helps children see the significance of these actions beyond their immediate effects.

Teaching gratitude and generosity is a continuous process that requires consistent effort from parents. By modeling, teaching directly, using stories, encouraging reflection, providing praise, creating traditions, and discussing impacts, parents can effectively instill these important values in their children. The result is not just a more pleasant home environment, but also the development of individuals who are more likely to contribute positively to their communities and society at large.

ᑭᑭᑭ

"Generosity in parenting goes beyond giving material things; it involves generously giving your time, attention, and patience, nurturing a relationship that grows deeper with each shared moment."

ᗡᗡᗡ

EIGHTEEN

CELEBRATING SUCCESSES AND LEARNING FROM FAILURES

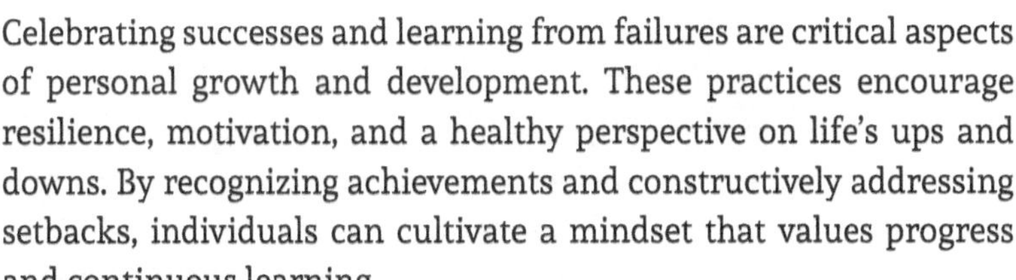

Celebrating successes and learning from failures are critical aspects of personal growth and development. These practices encourage resilience, motivation, and a healthy perspective on life's ups and downs. By recognizing achievements and constructively addressing setbacks, individuals can cultivate a mindset that values progress and continuous learning.

Celebrating successes, big or small, is essential because it reinforces positive behavior and achievements. When people take the time to celebrate, it not only boosts their confidence but also increases their motivation to pursue further goals. This is especially important for children, as it helps them develop a sense of self-worth and accomplishment. However, celebrating successes isn't just about acknowledging big milestones; it's equally important to recognize the small steps along the way. This might include praising a child for improving their grades, acknowledging an adult's commitment to a new fitness regime, or celebrating the completion of a small project at work. Recognizing these smaller achievements helps build momentum and encourages a consistent effort towards larger goals.

The way in which successes are celebrated also matters. Celebrations should be meaningful and reflect the nature of the achievement. For instance, a family might celebrate a child's good report card with a special dinner, or a team might celebrate the completion of a major project with an outing. The key is to make the celebration reflective of the personal significance of the achievement.

Conversely, learning from failures is equally important. Failure is an inevitable part of life and can provide valuable lessons if approached with the right mindset. Rather than viewing failures as a negative end point, they can be seen as opportunities for growth and improvement. This perspective helps individuals remain resilient in the face of setbacks and maintains their motivation to try again.

When dealing with failures, it is crucial to maintain a supportive and non-judgmental atmosphere. This is particularly important in a family or team setting, where the fear of criticism can prevent individuals from taking risks or trying new things. Instead, focus should be on what can be learned from the experience. Discussing what went wrong, why it went wrong, and what could be done differently next time are constructive ways to handle failure. This process not only leads to better future performance but also helps individuals and groups adapt and innovate.

Reflection is a powerful tool in both celebrating successes and learning from failures. Taking the time to reflect on what led to a success can help identify the actions and efforts that were most effective, which can be replicated in the future. Similarly, reflecting on failures can provide insights into the factors that need adjustment. Reflection should be an ongoing process, not reserved only for moments of success or failure but integrated into regular routines to continually improve and adjust strategies.

Encouragement plays a critical role in both scenarios. Encouraging words after a success can amplify the positive feelings associated with it, while encouragement after a failure can soften the blow and motivate individuals to continue striving towards their goals. It's important that encouragement is specific and sincere, focusing on the effort and improvement rather than just the outcome.

Setting a culture that values both success and failure as part of the learning process is crucial. In families, schools, and workplaces, creating an environment where individuals feel safe to experiment and take risks without fear of harsh judgment fosters creativity and innovation. It also builds a community where members support each other's growth through both triumphs and trials.

Celebrating successes and learning from failures are integral to personal and collective growth. These practices not only enhance motivation and resilience but also foster an environment of continuous improvement and support. By recognizing and valuing each step in the journey towards personal and communal goals, individuals and groups can thrive even in the face of challenges, ultimately leading to a more fulfilling and productive life.

ppp

"The art of parenting is never finished. Each day presents new challenges and opportunities to learn and grow alongside your child, creating a tapestry of shared experiences that binds you together."

ᗺᗺᗺ

NINETEEN

KEEPING CONNECTIONS STRONG AS KIDS GROW

Maintaining strong connections with children as they grow is essential for their emotional and social development. These connections provide a foundation of security and trust that supports children through various stages of growth and into adulthood. As children mature, the nature of parent-child relationships inevitably changes, but the importance of keeping these connections strong remains constant.

One of the primary ways to maintain a strong connection with growing children is through communication. Open, honest communication builds trust and helps children feel valued and understood. It's important for parents to listen actively to their children, showing genuine interest in their thoughts, feelings, and experiences. This means more than just hearing their words; it involves engaging with their emotions and showing empathy. As children grow older and face more complex life situations, having a reliable source of emotional support in their parents is invaluable.

Regular family time is another crucial element in keeping connections strong. Despite the busy schedules that come with growing children, setting aside dedicated time for family activities can have a profound impact on maintaining relationships. This could be as simple as having meals together, scheduling regular family game nights, or planning weekend outings. These moments provide opportunities for family members to bond and create lasting memories.

As children enter adolescence, they naturally seek more independence. It's important for parents to respect this need while still maintaining closeness. Striking the right balance between giving freedom and being involved can be challenging but is crucial for keeping connections strong. Parents can do this by setting clear boundaries that allow for increasing autonomy while ensuring safety and open lines of communication. This approach shows children that their parents respect their growing independence and trust their decision-making, which in turn strengthens the relationship.

In addition to spending quality time together, sharing interests and hobbies can also strengthen bonds. Parents might take an interest in their children's hobbies or share their own. Whether it's sports, music, reading, or any other activity, shared interests provide a natural and enjoyable way to connect and communicate. This doesn't mean parents have to intrude on every aspect of their child's interests, but showing support and genuine curiosity can encourage closer ties.

Emotional support is especially important as children face various challenges in life. Parents need to be approachable and available to discuss anything from academic pressures to personal relationships. Providing guidance while allowing children to make their own decisions helps them develop problem-solving skills and independence. Moreover, knowing they have a supportive home environment gives children the confidence to navigate life's challenges.

Acknowledging and celebrating achievements is another way to maintain strong connections. Celebrations not only mark milestones but also show children that their parents are paying attention and care about their successes. Whether it's academic achievements, personal accomplishments, or just small daily victories, recognizing and celebrating these moments can greatly enhance familial bonds.

Handling conflicts constructively is also essential. Disagreements and conflicts are natural, but how they are handled can either strengthen or weaken relationships. Parents should strive to resolve conflicts through dialogue and understanding rather than punishment or anger. This teaches children that conflicts can be resolved through communication and mutual respect, fostering a healthier relationship dynamic.

Finally, maintaining traditions can play a significant role in keeping family connections strong as children grow. Traditions, whether related to holidays, family outings, or even simple nightly rituals like reading a book together, create a sense of continuity and belonging. As children grow into adults, these traditions can become cherished memories and may even be passed down to the next generation.

Maintaining strong connections with children as they grow involves a mix of communication, shared activities, emotional support, and mutual respect for independence. By actively engaging in their lives and providing a stable foundation of love and support, parents can foster deep and enduring relationships with their children. These connections not only benefit the emotional and social development of children but also enrich the lives of parents, making the family unit stronger as a whole.

❦❦❦

"Ending the day with a peaceful bedtime routine is like gently closing the cover of a well-loved book. It's a moment to cherish the day's story, settle the pages, and rest before the dawn of a new chapter."

TWENTY

Reflecting on Your Parenting Journey

Reflecting on your parenting journey is a valuable exercise that helps you understand the impact of your actions, appreciate the growth of both your children and yourself, and guide future parenting decisions. Parenting is one of the most challenging and rewarding roles in life, and taking the time to reflect can enhance your effectiveness and enjoyment as a parent.

Reflection involves looking back at the experiences you've had, the decisions you've made, and the challenges you've faced. It allows you to celebrate successes, learn from mistakes, and recognize areas where you can improve. This reflective practice is not about being critical or judgmental but about approaching your experiences with curiosity and openness to growth.

One of the first steps in reflecting on your parenting journey is to acknowledge and appreciate the successes. This can include specific instances where you felt you handled a challenging situation well, times when you supported your children effectively, or simply moments when you enjoyed family life. Celebrating these successes can boost your confidence and motivation. It can also strengthen the bond with your children as they see and feel your joy and pride in their achievements and your own.

Reflecting on the challenges is equally important. Every parent faces difficulties, and it's normal to feel overwhelmed at times. By examining these challenging moments, you can gain insights into what might have triggered certain reactions in both you and your children. Understanding these triggers can help you manage similar situations better in the future. It's crucial to approach this aspect of reflection without guilt or regret but as an opportunity to learn and grow.

An effective way to engage in reflection is to keep a journal. Writing about your daily interactions, feelings, and thoughts can provide a detailed record of your parenting journey. Over time, reviewing this journal can reveal patterns and progress that might not be evident in the day-to-day. It can also serve as a personal outlet for expressing emotions and thoughts that you need to process privately.

Another reflective practice is to discuss your parenting experiences with others. This could be with a partner, friends, family members, or even a support group. Such conversations can provide different perspectives and supportive feedback. Hearing how others handle similar situations can offer new strategies or confirm that your experiences are normal and shared by many parents.

Self-reflection also involves considering the influence of your own upbringing on your parenting style. Many parents subconsciously adopt or react against the ways they were parented. By reflecting on how your experiences as a child affect your behavior as a parent, you can make more conscious choices about which practices to continue and which to change.

Setting aside time for regular reflection is important. This could be a quiet moment each evening, a weekly time set aside to review the past week, or a more formal monthly or annual review. The key is consistency, as regular reflection can lead to continuous improvement and deeper understanding.

Reflecting on your parenting journey also means recognizing the evolving nature of your role as your children grow. The needs of a toddler are vastly different from those of a teenager, and your parenting will need to adapt. Reflection can help you navigate these changes smoothly, ensuring that your parenting evolves in step with your children's development.

Conclusion, reflecting on your parenting journey is a powerful tool for personal growth and family harmony. It allows you to recognize and celebrate successes, learn from challenges, and continuously adapt your parenting practices to meet the changing needs of your children. By making reflection a regular part of your life, you ensure that your parenting is thoughtful, informed, and responsive, contributing to a nurturing and supportive family environment.

ϼϼϼ

"Every tantrum or tear is a message, a clue to your child's inner world. Responding with mindfulness and compassion helps decode these messages, guiding your child through their emotions and strengthening the trust between you."

TWENTY-ONE
SUMMARY

Parenting is a complex, rewarding journey that involves nurturing, teaching, and growing alongside your children. It encompasses a range of practices and techniques aimed at fostering healthy development and strong familial bonds. Each aspect of parenting contributes uniquely to the overall well-being of both children and parents, shaping the family dynamic and the individual characters within it.

Starting with the foundation of mindful parenting, it's essential to understand that being present and engaged in our interactions with children helps build a solid and secure emotional base. This presence reassures children that they are valued and supported, enabling open communication and fostering a deep sense of security and trust.

Recognizing the importance of being present, it's also crucial to practice active and empathetic listening. Listening with love means fully engaging with your child's feelings and experiences, which enhances communication and strengthens your relationship. Such deep understanding can significantly influence positive behavioral development and emotional intelligence.

As children grow, instilling a sense of compassion and patience in them—and practicing it ourselves—becomes vital. Compassionate parenting encourages children to be kind and considerate, while being patient teaches them about resilience and the importance of timing, helping them navigate life's challenges more effectively.

Self-care for parents is another critical aspect, often overlooked in the busy day-to-day life. Parents need to maintain their well-being to provide the best care and guidance for their children. A well-rested, healthy, and emotionally stable parent is better equipped to handle the demands of parenting.

Building emotional intelligence in children is not just about understanding and managing emotions but also about teaching them to interact positively with others. Emotional intelligence is a key predictor of personal and professional success, as it involves managing one's own emotions and understanding the emotions of others.

Creating a peaceful home environment sets the stage for every family member to thrive. This tranquility at home helps children feel safe and supported, promoting better learning and emotional well-being.

In terms of discipline, connecting rather than punishing can be more effective in teaching appropriate behavior. This approach respects the child's feelings and experiences, using understanding and communication to address behavioral issues.

The role of patience in parenting cannot be understated. It's a quality that not only helps manage children's behavior but also teaches them how to handle their own frustrations calmly.

As children become more independent, maintaining a connection becomes challenging but essential. It's important to balance giving freedom with ensuring that children still feel connected and supported by their family.

Starting each day with a mindful morning and ending with a serene bedtime routine can significantly influence the emotional tone of the household. These practices help children and parents manage their energy and emotions effectively.

Handling tantrums and emotional outbursts with mindfulness can transform challenging moments into opportunities for growth and learning, while emphasizing the importance of play enriches a child's learning and strengthens bonds through shared joy and creativity.

Teaching children about mindful eating and incorporating gratitude and generosity into daily life prepares them to make healthy choices and appreciate the good in their lives and in others.

Handling stress as a family unit strengthens relationships and teaches valuable coping mechanisms, while celebrating successes and learning from failures teaches resilience and appreciation for life's ups and downs.

Lastly, reflecting on the parenting journey helps parents stay mindful of their growth and challenges, ensuring that they continue to learn and adapt as their children grow.

ᐳᐳᐳ

Citation And Reference

This book represents the culmination of extensive research and meticulous analysis, incorporating a diverse range of sources, including numerous books, scholarly studies, and personal experiences. Additionally, I have scoured various websites to gather relevant information and data essential for the compilation of this work. I have taken every precaution to ensure the accuracy of the information presented and have diligently cited all sources to acknowledge their contributions.

Despite these efforts, the possibility of inadvertent errors remains. I deeply value the insights of my readers and appreciate any feedback that can help identify and rectify such inaccuracies. I encourage you to bring any discrepancies to my attention.

Your feedback is not only welcome but crucial, as it will aid in correcting current editions and enhancing the content of future ones. I am committed to maintaining the highest standards of accuracy and reliability in my work and thank you for your support and understanding.

Additionally, I firmly uphold the principle of freedom of speech and expression as guaranteed under Article 19(1)(a) of the Constitution of India, and I respect the diverse viewpoints and expressions of all readers.

ppp

Other Books Of The Author

1. Empowering Minds: A Journey into Women's Self-Discovery and Power
2. The Dynamics of Motivation: Catalyzing Thought into Action
3. Meditation and Mental Well Being: The Path to Inner Peace and Clarity
4. The Psychology of Child Education: Nurturing Future Generations
5. Ethical Enlightenment: A Modern Guide to Living with Integrity
6. Voices of Empowerment: Stories of Women Rising Against Odds
7. Social Psychology in Everyday Life: Understanding Human Connections
8. The Essence of Motivational Speaking: Inspiring Change in Others
9. Balancing Acts: Women, Work, and the Will to Lead
10. Guiding with Grace: Raising Children with Compassion and Awareness
11. The Power of Positive Aging: Embracing Life After Fifty
12. Building Resilient Communities: Social Work in Action
13. The Ethical Educator: Principles for Teaching and Learning
14. From Insight to Impact: Social Psychology for a Better World
15. The Ethics of Empathy: A Guide to Ethical Living
16. The Science of Empowering the Self: Navigating Life's Challenges with Psychological Wisdom
17. The Mindful Conscious Leader: Meditation Techniques for Modern Management
18. Pioneering Spirit: Women's Pathways to Leadership and Empowerment
19. Feeling to Healing: The Role of Emotional Intelligence in Child Development
20. Transformative Talks and Words of Inspiration: Insights into Motivational Oratory

❦❦❦

Contact

Dr. Minakshi Bansal
Social Activist
Ahmedabad, Gujarat, Bharat
minakshiindiag20@yahoo.com

❧❧❧

|| LOKAHA SAMASTHAHA SUKHINO BHAVANTU ||

• 133 •

9 798889 415598 2